JET
The Little Raccoon

By Richard Conyard

© Jet The Little Raccoon
ISBN:978-1-989755-10-5
copyright 2022 by Richard Conyard

All rights reserved
This book or any portion there of may not be reproduced or used, in any manner what so ever, without the express written permission of the Author / Photographer.
Except for the use of a brief quotation in book reviews.

I am a little bit naughty

Do you know what kind of animal I am?

Play Date

We live in a big forest in a big tree,
next to the sea

Mummy teaches us to climb

**Oh no,
I think I went
too high!**

There are lots of fun secret paths to explore

Mummy Teaches us how to fish in the pool

sunflower seeds please

We play a game
and find
the
hidden snacks

My Mum , says I must eat all my dinners, so that I will grow big and strong and have a thick shiny coat

This is Boo, my little sister

What animals are we?

Meet
Push
And
Shove
The
Stripes
Brothers

Our friends the stripes brothers are very small and fluffy

but they have a BIG smell

These are some of the other animals who live around us

These are the answers to guessing the animals

- 1. Red Squirrel
- 2. Nuthatch.
- 3. Bluejay.
- 4. Hare.
- 5. Hummingbird.
- 6. Chipmunk

How many did you know?

**I have to say goodbye now
Winter will be here soon**

**When the wind blows and the snow falls
I like to stay at home and sleep for a while**

**On sunny winter days you may see me
playing in the snow**

Dedicated to my two wonderful sons
Johnny & Kai

And Jet and the lovely creatures of the wood

Photographer and Author Richard Conyard
Cover & book design Sharan Arnold

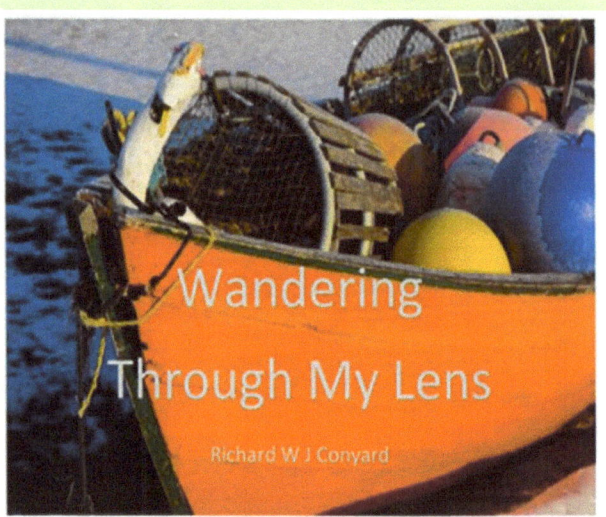

Other books :

**Wandering Through My Lens: P.E.I
(Available on Amazon)**

Follow on:

Tik Tok@richardconyard715
   Follow Jet, his friends & family on daily videos
   (family friendly Tik Tok channel)

Youtube@A Deck Full of Cute and Cuddly Critters

Picfair@Richard W J Conyard

Redbubble.com Richard W Conyard

www.ingramcontent.com/pod-product-compliance
Lightning Source LLC
Chambersburg PA
CBHW061403090426
42743CB00003B/130